"This book will be treasured by thousands of us who want our country to keep the beauty of the landscape as we remember it . . . and to leave this splendor for our grandchildren."

For Bob Leslie —
happy wildflower adventures!

Lady Bird Johnson

Number Seven:
The Louise Lindsey Merrick Texas Environment Series

To Bob —

Frank Lively Apr. 1984

Jack C. Lewis

Tommie Pinkard

Bob Burns

TEXAS IN BLOOM

TEXAS IN BLOOM

Photographs from *Texas Highways* Magazine

Introduction by GLEN EVANS

Foreword by LADY BIRD JOHNSON

Preface by FRANK LIVELY

and TOMMIE PINKARD

TEXAS A&M UNIVERSITY PRESS   College Station

Library of Congress Cataloging in Publication Data
Main entry under title:

Texas in bloom.

(The Louise Lindsey Merrick Texas environment series;
no. 7)
Includes index.
1. Wild flowers—Texas—Identification. 2. Wild flowers—
Texas—Pictorial works. 3. Texas highways—Illustrations.
I. Evans, Glen L. (Glen Louis), 1911–   . II. Texas
highways. III. Series.
QK188.T28 1984   582.13'09764   83-40500
ISBN 0-89096-180-8

The assistance of Geyata Ajilvsgi, Herbarium Botanist, Department
of Biology, Texas A&M University, and of Victor H. Treat, Assistant
Professor of History, Texas A&M University, in the preparation of
this book is gratefully acknowledged.

Manufactured in the United States of America
FIRST EDITION

CONTENTS

FOREWORD

Texas in bloom! Is there a more heartlifting sight?

Since time began, travelers as well as those of us who live here and glory in the seasons have struggled to make our words live up to the sea of bluebonnets, the sunshine stand of Indian blankets mixed with yellow coreopsis, the timid winecup peeping out of a limestone bank.

The journal of Texas Rangers riding through fields of wild flowers brushing their horses stirrup-high, letters of an early governor's wife, Lucadia Pease, describing the prairies after a rain—these are the written history of what our landscape has been.

Kipling's words come to mind:

Something lost behind the ranges,
Something hidden, go and find it.
Go and look behind the ranges,
Lost and waiting for you. Go.

The thresholds of beauty continue to lure us into the outdoors, to the trails and country roads and now along the concrete ribbons that stretch across miles and miles of Texas.

Each year I try to save spring for wild flowers and me, circling my calendar late March and April and May and writing firmly across, "Hold for wild flower season!" I resent the intrusions that inevitably come, for I am selfish about that time when what I want most to do is ride and ride or walk and walk and feast my eyes upon the wonders of the Lord and the help provided by the Texas Highway Department. They made peace years ago, with the encouragement and applause of citizens, and are now holding off the mowing to give the wild flowers time to leave their seeds for another spring.

Each part of Texas has its glory roads. When the rains come, you can drive through bright colors on the Texas High Plains, with white blooms of the Mexican poppy, down across the Hill Country of bluebonnets and Indian paintbrush and thousands of their flowering kinsmen, and into the shaded landscapes of East Texas, where the boughs of wild dogwood like white lace frame a field of black-eyed susans or blue cornflowers. The rights-of-way along the seventy-one thousand miles of these highways, to my mind, are the last citadel of nature's beauty where the public can enjoy Texas in bloom.

I read hungrily the words of Lucadia Pease, writing back East in April, 1854, about the brand new state where her husband had brought her to share the governor's mansion: "The prairies are gay with flowers. We gathered some bouquets of the annual phlox which is very abundant, covering whole fields, and the white flower which we call at home Scotch thistle, a foxglove very pretty, and a beautiful lily with a bulbous root. Austin is said to look prettier now than at any other season of the year. The trees are in full leaf and wildflowers are abundant."

I relish again the words of our famous naturalist Roy Bedichek, who liked to give human qualities to the birds and flowers he described: "Flowers were everywhere. A few stood up bravely on exposed ledges; some sought the protection of rugged boulders which were pausing for a few centuries or more on their way down the hill; others lux-

uriated in seepy depressions which detained sediment. Here, blooming cheerily, among the toughest and most presumptuous was the blue gilia, well named golden-eye, delicate and coquettish. It does seem a miracle that from the bones of tiny organisms deposited millions of years ago on the floor of an ancient sea, there should now arise to greet the sun, a little flower marked by such ingenious and beautiful workmanship."

Will nature's bouquets of the seasons so freely spread be lost to the encroaching cities? Never will we need them more to feed our soul! That is one thing our National Wildflower Research Center here in Austin was created to do: further the use of wild flowers, plants, and shrubs in public areas—highway rights-of-way, city parks, and perhaps even industrial parks.

I am glad this book has been published by the Texas A&M University Press. That great university has been carrying the message of the land to citizens for 108 years and is still at it through its classrooms and greenhouses and far-reaching press. The Texas Highway Department has translated the message into action and into magnificent pictures that say more than a thousand words. This book, *Texas in Bloom*, will be treasured by thousands of us who want our country to keep the beauty of the landscape as we remember it in our youth (for me this goes back half a century) and to leave this splendor for our grandchildren.

LADY BIRD JOHNSON

PREFACE

Photographer Jack Lewis looked approvingly at the field of bluebonnets studded with bright red Indian paintbrush. An old rusty hay rake gave the scene just the right touch. He put his eye to the glass of his view camera and pulled the black cloth over his head. Patiently, he checked focus, light, and composition. He shifted the camera slightly and went over every detail, concentrating on the image he saw through the lens. Finally he was ready to insert the film. He removed the black cloth and looked up in surprise. Around him he counted fifteen people, all with tripods and cameras, all trying to get the same photograph.

Jack has encountered situations like this often during the past twenty years. Aspiring photographers, not always on organized tours, will follow the *Texas Highways* cameraman and try to emulate his success as a landscape photographer.

Jack's landscapes, especially those of spring wild flowers, have helped make *Texas Highways* magazine popular with hundreds of thousands of people throughout the world. In fact, the April issue each year is traditionally devoted to wild-flower photographs, especially of bluebonnets. And it has proved to be the most popular issue of each year.

Wild flowers can be counted among the state's top visitor attractions. In the spring thousands of Texans and pilgrims from other states drive many thousands of miles to enjoy the blossoms that brighten our roadsides and blanket our fields. The State Department of Highways and Public Transportation helps make this spring show the success it is each year. For more than fifty years the department has been sowing wild-flower seeds and cultivating other plants along the highways and in

the roadside parks. The department has more than one million acres planted in grasses, trees, shrubs, and wild flowers. Now selected areas are being allowed to return to their natural state, but the department will always maintain the wild flowers so motorists can enjoy the splashes of springtime color.

Texas Highways magazine, published monthly by the Travel and Information Division of the State Department of Highways and Public Transportation, devotes many of its pages each year to showing and telling its readers about the department's role in propagating wild flowers as well as in preserving other natural beauties of the state. Before May, 1974, *Texas Highways* had been a departmental magazine emphasizing highway design, construction, and maintenance. But since that date its new mission has been to show Texans and the rest of the world just how beautiful the Friendship State is. In the past ten years *Texas Highways* has told the story of the state in word and picture, with articles on its history, its people, its changing environment, its natural resources. If the magazine has gained a reputation for one strong suit, that has to be for its publication of spectacular photographs showing the state's natural beauty.

A number of talented photographers have contributed their skills to producing those pictures, many of which are reproduced on the following pages. *Texas Highways* would like to thank the following for making this book possible: Randy Green (on our staff), Bob Parvin (former staffer), division photographers Jack Lewis and Greg White, and John Suhrstedt (retired).

We offer these photographs as only a sam-

pling of Texas' beauty. Since our state has more than five thousand species of wild flowers, *Texas Highways* magazine has many years—and many books—to go before it will have covered all of them. We hope to be back with another book in the near future.

FRANK LIVELY
TOMMIE PINKARD
Texas Highways

INTRODUCTION

It's not something one would care to dwell on at length, but for a very long time—throughout most of its geologic history, in fact—Texas was never in bloom. In those dark days it was totally destitute of flowers; it had not even a dogwood blossom to herald the coming of spring in its pineywoods region, nor a solitary bluebonnet to second that announcement from deep in the heart of Texas. Actually, that was during the eons of earth's history before the age of flowering plants had begun. No flowers then bloomed anywhere else in the world, either.

When in the overall scheme of things the time had come for flowering plants to arrive on earth, they had to compete for living space with more primitive nonflowering kinds that had long since become well established. They probably had to endure destructive foraging by ravenous plant-eaters, too, for this all took place back in Cretaceous times when the awesome plant-eating dinosaurs, along with their meat-eating relatives, were still the lords of the earth. It seems remarkable that flowering plants ever managed to gain a foothold under such conditions. But gain it they did—gained it and over succeeding epochs gradually expanded their range, diversifying as they did so into various specialized kinds to fit the conditions of the different habitats they encountered. They were irresistible. In time they colonized the world. And by that time they had become an extended family encompassing thousands of different species of flowering trees, shrubs, vines, forbs, and grasses.

So when man—at some unspecified but much later time—finally put in his appearance, those plants provided him with an abundant variety of comestibles in the form of roots, flowers, seeds, nuts, and fruits. He could not have survived without them, and to this day neither could we.

The flowering plants are indeed vital to our physical existence, but we need them as well for our spiritual and mental welfare. They charm our senses, stimulate our minds, and enliven our spirits. We need them to restore our faith in miracles, when their long-dormant seeds suddenly spring forth as vigorous and beautiful plants. And we need them to remind us that although "beauty is its own excuse for being," a thing of beauty can also have incalculable practical value. Finally, we need wild flowers as a good and sufficient excuse for taking to the woods and fields, if only for a pleasant morning outing.

In their excellent guidebook *Roadside Flowers of Texas*, Mary Motz Wills and Howard S. Irwin advised their readers that "a full understanding and appreciation of wildflowers can come only with study." And they explain their objective: "It is our goal rather to encourage an intelligent interest in Texas wildflowers than to stimulate purely sentimental rapture."

Clearly, what the authors meant by "study" was not perusal of smatterings of general information relating to wild flowers—such as that which might be gleaned from these pages. They had in mind, rather, a more disciplined scholarly approach. Starting with a glossary of botanical terms with which to learn the scientific names of a flower's various parts,

one should then familiarize oneself with the use of identification keys and proceed to identify the unknown species likely to be encountered. And this is obviously a sound procedure for those who intend to make a profession, or even a serious avocation, of botany, or any of its related fields such as forestry or horticulture. Certainly the pleasures to be derived from a studious approach to wild flowers by a person with a studious cast of mind are as legitimate as any other—and quite possibly in the long run more rewarding. For that person there is joy in learning itself, and since there is no end to what remains to be learned, he or she can spend a lifetime in this ever-satisfying pursuit.

But such a scholarly approach has little or no appeal for most people who care about flowers. Rather than undertake a disciplined study, they will gladly settle for something less than "a full understanding and appreciation." Many will even settle for some of that "purely sentimental rapture" that Wills and Irwin seem to disparage. And if they seem somewhat indifferent about where a flowering species fits into the Linnaean system of classification, that does not necessarily mean that they are also indifferent to the flower's intrinsic beauty and fragrance or to its ability to inspire a poem or a painting or a fine photograph.

Walt Whitman, the great American poet, would not have agreed with the advice of Wills and Irwin; he had cautionary words *against* their suggestion: "You must not know too much, or be too precise or scientific about birds and trees and flowers and water-craft; a certain free margin, and even vagueness— perhaps ignorance, credulity—helps your enjoyment of these things."

Well—but there are different kinds of enjoyment. Whitman's words must have been directed to those who care deeply only for the aesthetic's value of things, for the "sense of wonder" to be derived from seeing and contemplating a thing of beauty. They certainly don't apply to the scientist who finds much pleasure and gratification in his work. He doesn't fret about the danger of "knowing too much." His worry is that he can never know enough. Nor do they apply very much to people of my cast of mind. My view is that the "sense of wonder" is destroyed not by knowing too much about a thing but by too much familiarity with it. A spectacular sunset, seen once or twice in a year, makes your heart jump, even if you know all about the meteorological phenomena that cause it. But seen every day for months on end, it assuredly will lose its appeal, regardless of what you know, or don't know, about it.

It doesn't diminish my admiration of a beautiful lotus blossom to know that it is the national flower of India or that its flattened central receptacle is full of delicious and nutritious nutlike seeds. My pleasure at looking upon a noble oak isn't sullied by the knowledge that it sprang from an acorn, which quite possibly was buried centuries ago by a squirrel hoarding his winter supply of nuts. Are we to suppose that it hurts anyone's enjoyment of our sometimes glorious fields of bluebonnets because he or she happens to have learned somewhere that their roots harbor nitrogen-fixing bacteria, and thereby contribute enrichment to the soil, or that they, unlike many field flowers with which they are often associated, must start growing in the autumn before their spring flowering season—or because he or she remembers from grammar school that the bluebonnet is the Texas state flower?

The yuccas, flowering year after year, sometimes live to a ripe old age on the order of sixty or seventy years. The Trecul yucca, or Spanish dagger, of the southern part of the state and the Torrey yucca of the Trans-Pecos region are among our most reliable midwinter

bloomers. I am tempted to reveal here that, unlike nearly all other flowering plants, the yuccas are *not* promiscuous. They are pollinated at night—but only, I hasten to add, by the female *Pronuba* moth. How she deliberately collects pollen from one flower and applies it, after depositing an egg in the ovary, to the stigma of another, thus fertilizing the latter, makes a fascinating story about the absolute interdependency between a kind of insect and a kind of plant. But it isn't because of fear of destroying the reader's interest in yuccas by teaching too much about them that I refrain from trying to tell the story in full.

Scientific names of plants present a similar problem. Botanists, of course, use the scientific names not only to be more precise in meaning than they can be with folk names but also to be understood by the international community of scientists, which certainly does not use the same folk names. Flower fanciers other than those of botanical persuasion, however, usually find the scientific names unspellable, unpronounceable, and unrecallable. They much prefer the familiar folk names, which seem more descriptive and are easier to spell and remember.

From looking at a dense, shoulder-high thicket, which from some distance away appears as if it just received a frosting of new snow, you would know soon enough how it got the folk name of "whitebrush." And closer up, where the whole thicket seems strangely animated with a kind of ecstatic wriggling and twitching as hosts of buzzing and droning honeybees scramble over the tiny white blossoms avidly gathering their cargo, you would understand why it is also known, equally aptly, as "beebrush." At neither place would you have any clue why botanists call the shrub *Aloysia gratissima*.

"The botanists," wrote Roy Bedichek, "assign fearsomely cumbrous names, sometimes two or three, each cluttered up with the name of the individual who fathered it, and they are all duly frozen in print for the great convenience of scientists scattered about over the world; but you can't use these names in flesh and blood conversations." If, somewhere in West Texas, you should for the first time come upon a healthy clump of what looked to you much like prairie grass, except that it was bearing pretty blue terminal flowers—not what one expects to find on grasses—you might pause to admire and exclaim in wonderment over it and ask, "What in the world is this?"

"It's a blue-eyed grass," one companion might reply.

"Not a grass at all," the other, who happens to be a botanist, might respond, "It's *Sisyrinchium demissum*, a member of the iris family."

The next time you happened upon this pretty little plant in bloom, you would remember it not, I think, by its "fearsomely cumbrous" scientific name, but only as blue-eyed grass. Yet in the issue of scientific versus folk names it is not a matter of one or the other—not a matter of which is best. Each has its purpose. They are, in effect, elements of different languages. By all means, use the one that suits *your* purpose.

Wild flowers, like works of art, mean different things to different people. One afternoon on a fine spring day some years ago, I pulled up on the side of a quiet rural road in the Hill Country of central Texas where a spectacular patch of wild flowers in the adjacent pasture had captured my attention. The flowers, as I recall, included fireweed gaillardias, *Thelespermas*, white prickly poppies, and perhaps others, all seemingly at the peak of floral perfection. Delighted at the prospects

of getting some fine photographs, I took my camera from the car and spent the next thirty minutes or so exposing a lot of film.

Still reluctant to leave the patch of fragrant loveliness after finishing the photographing, I stood for a while with my arms resting on a fencepost, just soaking up the life-renewing essence of spring, and presently became aware that an approaching pickup was slowing to a stop behind me.

As the lean, middle-aged man in a sweat-stained Stetson and worn boots emerged from the pickup, his clothes, looks, and manner announced that he was a cowman. He walked over to where I was standing, nodded, and asked in a neighborly manner, "Got some car trouble?"

"No, thanks—no trouble," I said, "just stopped to look around for a while—and take a few pictures."

His gaze took in the camera hanging by its strap from my shoulder, then swept over the surroundings as if to decide what it was I had seen fit to photograph. I noticed that his eyes passed by the patch of flowers without a flicker but came to a focus on a grassy slope to my right, where a bunch of cows with their baby calves cavorting about them were grazing in our direction. Then his head nodded slowly.

"Bet you got some good ones," he said, "Nothing much makes a prettier picture than fat cows grazing on green grass."

I decided it might be best not to reveal that I had been so preoccupied with the flowers that until that moment I hadn't even noticed the cattle. Instead, I remarked about the fine seasonable weather we were having and how good it was to see grass starting up again, now that the drouth seemed to be broken at last.

"Yes," he agreed, "Grass's coming on real good right now—except where the weeds are choking it out."

"Weeds?" I asked.

"Yeah, there's lots of 'em, and they're growing mighty rank in places this year—like that bunch yonder," he said, nodding at last towards my patch of wild flowers.

Weeds! He called those lovely blossoms weeds!

I was astonished at that bit of blasphemy, but shouldn't have been. It should have occurred to me immediately that because he worked day after day among wild flowers, they had naturally ceased being a marvel to him—had even ceased to attract his notice. Moreover, being a cowman, he could be expected to have an almost reverent regard for grass and a corresponding irreverence for anything that interfered with its growth. Doubtless he would have agreed with whoever it was that described "weeds" as "plants growing where you want something else to grow." And now wild flowers were growing where he wanted good grass to grow, so, to him, perforce, they were weeds.

In my growing-up days on the farm, we did the very same thing. When such wild plants as morning glory, nightshade, sensitive brier, devil's claw, and bull nettle invaded our gardens and fields—as they did every year—we had to clear them out by hand with weeding hoes, which was onerous, palm-blistering labor, to prevent them from damaging our desperately needed crops. We despised those plants, spoke of them contemptuously as "weeds," and refused to admire their sometimes lovely blossoms, even when they were growing harmlessly along some unused roadside or fencerow.

The common dandelion in blossom is probably every bit as attractive as many of our well-regarded native wild flowers, yet nearly everyone regards it and treats it not as a flower to be admired but as an especially troublesome weed. And, considering its annoying affinity for fine lawns and gardens, it deserves

that epithet, just as a chicken-stealing skunk deserves to be called a varmint. Even so, it is a truly remarkable plant. With man's unintended assistance it has spread over the civilized world from its original base in southeastern Europe. It is as tough as rawhide and incredibly adaptable, and it seems to be at home wherever it lands. In North America, for instance, it flourishes as well in Canada's frigid prairie provinces as on our subtropical Gulf coastal plain. The dandelion is even said to be capable of self-pollination. If so, it can apparently go on flourishing forever—and with never a worry about the possibility of something bad happening to the pollinating insects. You will never see dandelions on the list of endangered species, though that is small comfort to keepers of well-groomed lawns.

I know a lady who cherishes the fine stands of native bluebonnets and verbenas that appear in favorable growing seasons in her vacant, untilled lot. But for some reason she abhors as "weeds" the handsome evening primroses that always appear with them. To me the primroses are quite attractive in themselves and complement the other flowers nicely, but they offend her, and she proceeds to rip them out.

I am fond of sunflowers. They remind me of my boyhood home and other pleasant places. I like their robustness and the way their big, bold flowers look me squarely in the face as I stand between them and the early sun, watching honeybees exploring their nooks and crannies. And I like the mourning doves and other pretty seed-eating birds that flock to the lavish caches of seeds the sunflowers leave behind after their flowering stage has passed. But many condemn sunflowers as weeds, for the usual good reasons, and others call them our most prosaic flowers. Vincent Van Gogh didn't think them prosaic. He saw their beauty, and captured it for posterity in a simple still life called "Sunflowers"

which must be one of the most admired flower paintings in the western world. Maybe the way to see elusive beauty in a flower is to study it with the intensity of an artist preparing to paint it.

In calling attention to a photograph of the graceful winter rosette of a Texas filaree in his excellent guidebook *Wildflowers of the Davis Mountains and the Marathon Basin, Texas,* Dr. Barton Warnock reminds us that "Plants do not have to be in flower to be beautiful." He is right, of course, though a plant is usually at its most beautiful stage when in flower. We need to be reminded that natural beauty takes many forms, and we shouldn't be unmindful of it, whatever form it takes.

Some plants—of both flowering and non-flowering kinds—have inherent beauty of form, an eye-pleasing arrangement of their various parts that needs no seasonal embellishment to capture one's admiration. And it is no disparagement of the flowering kinds to note that sometimes fruits or foliage enhance their beauty as much as or more than flowers, or that the combined effect of foliage and flowers is sometimes more pleasing than either of them viewed separately. That strange, drouth-loving member of the pineapple family, known familiarly as false agave and to science as *Hechtia scariosa*, is one example of a native plant whose colorful perennial form often eclipses the beauty of its seasonal blossom. Given adequate growing space, its numerous succulent red-tinged leaves, spine-tipped and thorn-rimmed, flare out into a nearly perfect rosette two or three feet in diameter so that the mature plant in itself looks like a spectacular giant-sized flower.

I have seen false agave growing in several places along the Rio Grande in the vicinity of Laredo and as far downstream as Falcon Reservoir, but fortunately it is most abundant upstream in the Big Bend National Park, where

it is protected by law from those who make a commercial business of gathering such unusual and attractive desert plants for sale in the rock garden trade.

The Texas mountain laurel, *Sophora secundiflora*, one of the two or three most beautiful and most popular native Texas shrubs, is a delight to look upon any day of the year. Its pleasing rounded shape and dense growth of glossy evergreen leaves make it an outstanding ornamental shrub on the basis of foliage alone. But in late March and April, when the great clusters of fragrant, violet-colored blossoms appear against a background of that elegant foliage, it is truly in its season of glory. And even after the flowers are spent, the big, silvery seed pods they spawned seem to add a pleasing touch to the plant's appearance. The hard, pea-sized, coral-red beans (sometimes maroon or yellow), which contain a powerful intoxicant, were once an article of commerce. Strung as beads, or ground to a powder, they were reportedly in brisk demand among the Indians—the beads for personal adornment, the powder for spicing up the mescal when the men decided to go on a glorious drunk. It is no mere coincidence that some of the laurel's other folk names are "mescal bean" and "big drunk."

Scattered thinly over much of the state, mountain laurel occurs most commonly on the limestone hills of the Edwards Plateau region. It is a prominent element of the woods on the upper slopes of the Mount Bonnel overlook in Austin, Texas—an especially convenient place to observe it.

Yaupon holly, *Ilex vomitoria*, is another evergreen native shrub (sometimes a small tree twenty or more feet tall) that graces its surroundings throughout the year, although its small, pale green blossoms are scarcely noticeable and do nothing to enhance its beauty. But around Christmastime the yaupon makes itself appropriately festive with a wealth of brilliant red berries among its shiny evergreen leaves. Unlike most of our decorative shrubs, it achieves its crowning glory in winter instead of spring, and with berries instead of blossoms.

To me, no new foliage is lovelier to look upon than the gracefully drooping, feathery, pale green leaves of honey mesquite when they first appear in the spring. But a little later on, when creamy catkinlike blossoms appear amidst the leaves and fill the air with their pervasive fragrance, the total effect on the senses is even more delightful. Unlike flowering dogwood, redbud, or huisache, which are justly famous for their flowers alone, and whose profusion of elegant blossoms usually appears before their leaves are much in evidence, mesquite blossoms are not lavish enough to carry the show on their own; they *need* the support of fancy foliage just as the foliage benefits by theirs.

Flame-leaf sumac's midsummer clusters of small greenish white flowers contribute something but not much to the shrub's generally good appearance. But in autumn, when its leaves and fruit clusters turn crimson with bright accents of yellow and brown and gold, it is nothing short of spectacular, especially where it forms sizable clumps or thickets an acre or more in area. Like flame-leaf sumac, Virginia creeper is also usually at its most attractive stage in autumn when its leaves turn scarlet, for the vine's loose clusters of small greenish blossoms are entirely unremarkable.

The normally ungainly prickly pear has one season of attractiveness in the spring, when its flat oval pads are adorned with big yellow or orange blossoms, as beautiful as those of the rose, and another in the waning days of summer, when the deep green pads are studded by fig-sized red or purple tunas. At which season is it most appealing? Poets

and connoisseurs, I suppose, and nectar-feeding insects surely, would choose its spring display of blossoms, while some of our border people, and a great variety of wildlife, who know the virtue of prickly pear fruit, might well prefer it when the ripe tunas are fat and savory.

There is not much doubt about when the always hungry Cabeza de Vaca would have preferred the prickly pear. He had a great deal of experience with that plant during his six years (1528–34) on the Texas coast, but never once in his journal did he mention its blossoms. Like the Indians who held him captive, however, he greatly cherished the ripened tunas. They were, in fact, what made possible his escape, for he and his three companions made their break during "the season of prickly pears," for then there was "food in the country side." The tunas sustained them until they finally encountered friendly tribes who supplied them with other food and assisted them on their way. Cabeza de Vaca's account is a priceless document of earliest Texas history. But for the prickly pear tunas, we might never have had it.

Despite the prickly pears' formidable "self-protection" of glochids and spines, deer, coyotes, wild turkeys, quail, and various other wild things avidly devour the tunas. "It is one of the sights of the Rio Grande," wrote Captain John Bourke, "to come suddenly upon a large, patriarchal, white goat with beard and breast dyed a blood red, from the juice of the tuna, and nostrils filled with the thorns of the fruit and leaf." Javelinas can subsist indefinitely on the succulent pads, which they eat freely, spines and all. Cattle and other livestock also eat the spiny food when better fare is lacking.

In Mexico, and to some extent in South Texas, many people relish not only the ripe tunas but also the *nopalitos*—the tender young pads before they have developed spines

or glochids. Both fruits and pads are articles of commerce and are sold in many of our grocery stores—especially those along the border.

Most of our herbaceous wild flowers are highly responsive to rainfall—not only to the total amount, but also to its seasonal distribution. Some spring bloomers such as bluebonnets and buttercup evening primroses are known as winter annuals because their seeds germinate in the fall and the plants grow slowly throughout the winter. These and other winter annuals require adequate fall and winter moisture to produce well at flowering time. Don't expect a bumper crop of bluebonnets or buttercups following a dry fall and winter, even in a very rainy spring.

But such a wet spring is all that is needed for a magnificent flowering of many regular annuals, such as gaillardias and Drummond phlox. Their seeds may have lain dormant in the soil for several years waiting for the right combination of spring moisture and temperature to trigger their genetic timing mechanism. When that happens, the seeds sprout, plants spring forth, blossoms open, pollinating insects promptly come calling, and fertilized ovules develop into seeds. Then, having fulfilled their destiny all within a single growing season, the plants die and make room for others.

It is astonishing how long the seeds of wild flowers can lie dormant in the soil and still be able to sprout and grow when favorable weather conditions finally arrive. During the great Dust Bowl drouth of the 1930's, large areas of bone dry, shifting sands in the southern Llano Estacado lay for years on end barren of any visible plant life. But after the drouth was finally broken by the record rains of 1941 there was suddenly an unbelievable proliferation of many kinds of wild flowers. They sprang up everywhere—in pastures and fields

and fencerows—and, incredibly, even spread blankets of exuberant colors across large areas of what had seemed for years to be completely barren and sterile dune fields. Never have I seen a more flamboyant floral display.

The seeds from which those flowers sprang had waited many years—no one can say just how many—for a chance to play out their destined role. But when the chance finally came, they responded with vigor and made up in part for the long, drab years of waiting.

In an article in the *Austin American-Statesman*, Mr. Carroll Abbott of Kerrville made an observation which has an important bearing on the durability of bluebonnet seeds. According to the account, a couple bought a fifty-year-old house, originally built on a foundation of cedar posts, and tore it down, intending to build a new one on the site. But for economic reasons they were delayed for a time from doing so. And then, according to Abbot, "On the spot where the house had stood, bluebonnets grew up in the exact pattern of the floor plan of that old house." As he explained it, the seeds from bluebonnets growing on the site when the house was built had lain dormant for half a century until the house was removed and the soil they rested in was again exposed to sun and rain.

Permanent swamps and bogs, notably those of the Big Thicket in Southeast Texas, are the essential habitat of some of our most beautiful and rare wild flowers. These, presumably, are not much affected by periodic variations in rainfall, though they might suffer considerably from prolonged freezing weather. Flowering trees and shrubs also—especially those of humid East Texas, such as magnolia, flowering dogwood, red buckeye, and redbud—seem not much affected by seasonal or annual variations in rainfall, so their blossoming time can usually be predicted. Not so, however, several shrub species of the drier

parts of the state, such as cenizo, whitebrush, and desert willow, which have made a remarkable adaptation to dryness and erratic timing of rainfall. They do not bloom on a genetically determined seasonal schedule, like cherries or peaches or most native plants, but instead wait for rain, whether it comes in spring, summer, or fall. And depending upon the frequency of rainfall, or on the complete lack of it, they will blossom several times in a year, or not at all.

After a drouth-breaking rain, anytime from April to November, fine stands of cenizo on caliche ridges in the brush country of South Texas adorn their silver white foliage with a profusion of pink to rose-colored blossoms and produce one of the finest wild-flower displays to be seen anywhere. But unfortunately—as any rancher in the region can tell you—drouth-breaking rains don't come often. And when they do come, most of those blossom displays will occur in remote places where nectar-feeding insects, but only a few people, or perhaps none at all, will have an opportunity to enjoy them.

The ocatillo, *Fouquieria splendens*, a desert shrub of the Trans-Pecos region, blooms in the spring like most flowering plants. But sometimes it blooms again in the summer in response to a soaking rain. Under such conditions in August and September I have seen a fine growth of ocatillos on the west slopes of the Quitman Mountains covered with bright crimson terminal clusters of flowers. This unusual and interesting shrub has multiple thorn-studded stems of approximately equal diameter and ten to fifteen feet tall. When the stems are cut from their base and set in the earth, they readily take root and grow. Rural Mexicans, by planting the stems very close together, make almost impenetrable living fences to protect their goats and poultry from predators. They also use the stems for fire-

wood and as a roofing material for shade arbors.

Many species of wild flowers can mature at very different sizes, which is worth remembering because the variations between the extremes can be so great that they confuse the identity of the plant. What we call their "normal" size is the size we are accustomed to seeing them at maturity and tends to reflect average habitat conditions. Under exceptionally favorable conditions, however, the same species may grow much larger than normal and be a great deal more fruitful, while under rigorous conditions it will reach maturity minimally fruitful and severely dwarfed.

In her delightful book *Land of Little Rain*, Mary Austin cites an instance of extraordinary variation in growth of a pigweed—or a relative thereof—because of radical change in moisture, and probably of temperature also, from one year to the next: "It is recorded in the report of the Death Valley expedition that after a year of abundant rains on the Colorado desert was found a specimen of *Amaranthus* ten feet high. A year later the same species in the same place matured in drought at four inches." A botanist recognized the identity of that dwarfed specimen; most of us would have passed it by without ever having noticed it. Or if we had seen it at maturity, would we have guessed that it belonged to a species capable of growing to thirty times that height?

In good soil on a vacant lot near my home, common sunflowers at this writing are seven or eight feet tall with fine, saucer-sized blossoms, while from sparse, rocky soil nearby, spindly but mature specimens of the same species are growing less than knee-high, with scraggly blossoms no larger than a silver dollar. In this case the size difference is entirely a result of differences in the fertility of the soils, for both areas receive the same amount of sunlight and moisture.

In *Karankaway Country*, Roy Bedichek tells how certain flowers along the Texas bayshore dunes have adapted to the adverse effects of battering coastal winds: "Delicate flowers—phlox, puccoons, daisies, asters, and many others—grow, bloom and seed right down against the ground. Common spiderwort, a plant two or three feet tall in central Texas, here attains a height of two or three inches, with flowers, however, as luxuriant as the species produces anywhere else." Apparently these plants have succeeded in drastically reducing their height in response to a single adverse environmental factor, the powerful winds, without losing or diminishing their seed-producing function—a most interesting example of adaptability, indeed.

Many of our showiest flowers flourish especially on undisturbed soils too thin and weak to support a stand of turf-forming grass; they also thrive on better soils that have been severely disturbed by erosion, road graders, plows, and the like. For that reason extensive colonies of such spring bloomers as pink evening primrose, white prickly poppy, horsemint, paintbrush, and bluebonnets are commonly seen in fallow fields and in the borrow trenches and ploughed fireguards bordering our highways and railroad rights-of-way. It is also why they are often found during their blossoming seasons and around abandoned garden plots and stock pens of old, falling-apart homesteads, where the original vegetation has been destroyed by overuse and abuse. It is no coincidence that such relics of bygone human tenancy as delapidated wagons, rusted farm implements, and moldering ruins of houses or sheds often appear in fine wild-flower photographs and paintings. Admittedly, a sense of the tragic always pervades these old abandoned places, but when the flowers are there, they are beautiful.

In seasonable weather you will not need to go looking for wild flowers, for then phlox, bluebonnets, paintbrush, *Thelesperma*, prairie verbena, gaillardia, and other colony-forming kinds break out in profusion in their respective seasons on prairies and open glades as well as on roadsides, in fields, and along fencerows. In such times you can enjoy floral extravagance with little exertion and be quite choosy about the flowers on which to lavish your attention, though you will miss all the fun that comes from searching in shady places for hidden patches of blossoms.

But when the land is wasting in drouth at the same blossoming seasons, few flowers will be in evidence. They will be largely confined to minor areas or niches where conditions are especially favorable. Species that formerly blanketed prairie slopes and ridges will be nearly or totally absent there. Look for them instead in local populations at the base of slopes, where semishaded alluvial soils have received moisture from slope runoff.

The first flowers of spring are apt to be found in sunny spots on south-facing stream banks, slopes, and bluffs. Being more exposed to sunlight there, the warmer soils expedite their early growth. In the Llano area of central Texas I have seen bright patches of bluebonnets in sequestered, south-facing nooks a full two weeks before the main bluebonnet population appeared.

As summer grows hotter and drier, most wild flowers disappear from view completely. For those who enjoy searching them out, a good place to look is in moist, shady spots along minor watercourses and around hillside seeps or springs. Among other worthwhile flowers likely to be found in such places is the ubiquitous *Commelina* dayflower, known also as widow's tears. It is one of several Texas flowers that continues to bloom practically throughout the frost-free months if plenty of shade and moisture are available.

This dayflower is one I remember fondly from childhood. To me, despite its ungainly stalk, its blossom is a thing of beauty. The two big blue petals—which must be the bluest blue in nature—open with the coming of morning light and spread gracefully outward to display their treasure, the bright little golden nuggets of pollen at their center. New blossoms open each morning, but they always close tightly at noon. "Morning flower," it seems, would be a better name than "dayflower."

Thomas Gray's much-quoted lamentation that "full many a flower is born to blush unseen and waste it's sweetness on the desert air" is fine poetry, but it doesn't do much for natural history. The blush doesn't go unseen, nor the fragrance undetected, just because no person happens to be on hand to savor them. Their blush and sweetness are not intended for him; we humans are merely unintentional beneficiaries of the flowers' charms. What that color and fragrance *are* intended for is, of course, an invitation to the nectar and pollen feeders. And the invitation, far from being "wasted on the desert air," is eagerly accepted by bees, butterflies, moths, ants, flies, beetles, hummingbirds, and hosts of other creatures. And they, in the course of feeding on the flower's proffered delicacies, perform a practical and enormously important function—they unintentionally transfer ovule-fertilizing pollen from a flower's anther to its, or to another flower's, stigma. Thus, the seed of procreation is made whole, and it now carries within itself the promise of a new generation of flowers to come.

I realize that the reader deserves a better explanation of the fascinating business of plant pollination than the overly simplified version above. And I wish I were able to explain the various and complicated ways plants perpetuate their kinds, but being confused, as I tend to be, about stigmas and stamens and pistils and things, and never being quite sure which

one does what to the other—or how—I am afraid I just couldn't quite carry it off. But before laying aside the subject of "the birds and the bees," I should note that watching the pollinators in action can be a most pleasurable experience, even if you don't know exactly what is going on. A most rewarding way for a flower fancier to spend an hour or two on a bright spring morning is to be knee-deep in some sweet-smelling wild-flower meadow, surrounded by beautiful flowers while hummingbirds, honeybees, and butterflies go about sampling nectar, each from the flowers of its choice. If you have ever wondered why butterflies are sometimes called "the winged flowers," watch such elegant ones as the red admiral, monarch, or tiger swallowtail flitting about among equally brightly colored blossoms, and you will soon have the answer.

As is widely known, hummingbirds are especially attracted to red flowers. Hence, those who enjoy watching the hummers—and who doesn't?—will do well to seek out such plants as Turk's cap, lantana, redbud, standing cypress, and red buckeye. The East Texas red buckeye in full flower seems to be an irresistible attraction; sometimes a dozen or more hummingbirds will be found feasting at the same time on a single shrub.

One of my memorable outdoor experiences involved an unplanned encounter with a variety of nectar-feeding birds. Back in the 1930's, the late Raymond W. Miller and I were camped for several days in Juniper Canyon in the Chisos Mountains, in what has since become the Big Bend National Park. All around camp was a fine stand of century plants, or magueys, many of which were already in bloom. They were the first I had ever seen, and I could scarcely believe my eyes. Their incredibly huge flowering stalks, all of which seemed to be nearly twenty feet tall, had fifteen or twenty alternating horizontal branches, each supporting a dinner-plate-sized spray of fragrant, cream-colored flowers.

Impressed as I certainly was by the handsome and stately plants in that spectacular mountain setting, I was even more fascinated by the number and variety of nectar-feeders swarming around their blossoms. There were, of course, hosts of bees and other insects on hand, but this time it was the hordes of feathered nectar-feeders that stole the show. I now think that their extraordinary concentration at that colony of blossoming plants was because of the absence of most of the usual spring flowers, which had failed to grow because of the then prevailing Dust Bowl drouth. The century plants, however, are not rain sensitive; they store moisture and nutrients throughout their ten- to twenty-year life in their crowns and succulent leaves. So when their flowering time comes, be the weather wet or dry, they pour their entire store of vital substance into their magnificent flowering stalks and blossoms—and then they die.

Hummingbirds were all over the place, in such numbers as I hadn't seen before, and haven't seen since. The familiar black-chinned species was the only one I recognized, but two or three unfamiliar Mexican species were also well represented.

Here, too, I had my first encounter with the magnificent band-tailed pigeon, a number of which were competing with the militant little hummers around the magueys' blossoms. The band-tails are our largest wild pigeons. They looked positively huge alongside the diminutive hummers. Unlike the hummers' hovering method of taking nectar, the pigeons perched themselves precariously on the edge of a flower spray, balancing when necessary by fluttering their wings, and simply inserted their beaks into one of the tubular flowers and sucked away until its supply of nectar was exhausted—drinking nectar in the same way that all pigeons and doves drink water, and quite unlike the way other birds drink.

Incongruous as it seems, it is in the driest part of the state—the north extension of the Chihuahuan Desert in the Trans-Pecos region—that worthwhile wild flowers are often found during a severe and widespread drouth. The reason, of course, is that a high percentage of desert plants are so adapted to dry conditions that they store up moisture in trunks and stems for use when none is available to their roots and curtail its use when moisture is scarce. These plants include the many species of cacti as well as ocatillo, sotol, the century plant, and several species of yucca. Among my favorites of these blossoming plants are the pitaya and claret-cup cacti, the century plant, ocatillo, and—especially—the Torrey yucca. The Torrey yucca—according to Barton Warnock, who knows the flowers of that region better than anyone else—can be seen blooming somewhere in the Trans-Pecos region every month of the year.

You will enjoy the outdoors more, not less, by being aware of the plants out there that can hurt you. Knowing how to recognize them and where they are likely to occur makes it a simple matter to avoid them, but only if you remain alert. Constant alertness in woods and fields prevents unnecessary hurts; it also sharpens your awareness and appreciation of everything else around you.

It is natural to want to touch or fondle things we find sensuously appealing, such as kittens and mink coats and attractive, soft-looking foliage. But it is risky business to try to pet a kitten that is arch-backed and spitting defiance, or to fondle a mink coat that is still being worn by a bad-tempered mink. And it is similarly unwise to heedlessly handle unfamiliar foliage that might be concealing needle-sharp spines or exuding a poisonous sap. Referring to its harsher side, Tennyson spoke of "Nature, red of tooth and claw," as indeed she often is. But her harshness can take the form of toxin and spine as well as "tooth and claw"; it comes clothed in foliage as well as fur and feathers.

Nature lovers often justify vegetal weaponry as "self-defense mechanisms," and I have no better name to propose for it. But certain "self-protected" plants will treat you harshly indeed, when you have no offensive intent whatsoever toward them, if through some ineptness or accident you are thrown into intimate contact with them or if, beguiled by the seeming caressability of their flowers or foliage, you gently attempt to stroke them. In either case you can come away with nasty thorn wounds or a painful rash from nettles or poison.

Many "naturally protected" plants, such as wild roses and dewberries, are not at all dangerous—only stand-offish. Their rather modest array of prickles is sufficient to prevent heavy-handed treatment but does not necessarily punish a knowing and gentle touch. Many others, including the different kinds of cacti, the spiny all-thorn shrub, and some kinds of locusts, give fair warning by prominent display of spines and thorns. Touch me at your own peril, those bristling armaments seem to say, so a reasonably cautious person isn't likely to be injured by them.

The plants to look out for are those that keep their defensive weaponry partly or completely concealed in leaves or flowers. In its blossoming season, huisache is surely one of our most striking, most fragrant, and most admired flowering trees or shrubs. It is the source of much superior honey in Texas. In France, and perhaps other European countries, it is cultivated by perfumeries, which extract the essence of fragrance from its blossoms. But—especially in its early growing stage—huisache branches bristle with viciously sharp thorns partly concealed in a feathery foliage that tempts familiarity. Moreover, it tends to grow in dense thickets

through which it is difficult to move without bumping into some spine-studded trunk or limb, and in that way it has inflicted many a painful injury to man and beast alike.

But the archvillain of the plant world is poison ivy—in all its three similar and equally virulent Texas varieties. It has caused more physical suffering, sometimes severe, and instilled more fear of venturing into the woods than all our other noxious plants combined. Yet nothing about it gives any hint or warning; it is in fact quite attractive, and in no way is it uncomfortable to the touch. Its so-called "self-protection" is a toxic oil which it exudes from all its parts. Instead of protecting itself from you, poison ivy spitefully punishes you later on for having dared to touch it. Those susceptible to its poison—and most people are, at least at some stage of their life—must learn to recognize it and avoid it or simply to stay away from wooded places where it might be growing. Unfortunately, it grows almost everywhere in wooded parts of the country. If there is nothing around for it to climb upon, it will make out very well as a shrub. If trees or posts or buildings are available for it to cling to, it will assume the form of a vine—and there is almost no limit to how high it will climb.

Poison ivy's distinctive trifoliate leaf makes it easy to identify by any boy or girl scout who takes the trouble to memorize what it looks like. But it has a fiendish way of concealing its identity among harmless leaves of trees and of somewhat similar vines, such as the Virginia creeper. And after its leaves are shed, the inconspicuous naked vines—which are quite as virulent as the leaves—are much more difficult to identify. As Russell Baker said in a newspaper column, "Be cautious about embracing nature too closely, especially if it is entwined around a tree trunk."

Bull nettle, known to Mexicans as *malo mujer*, or "evil woman," and to botanists as *Cnidoscolus texanus*, produces admirable clusters of fragrant white blossoms. Even so, it should be high on every outdoor person's list of absolutely unpettable plants. Unlike poison ivy, it favors the open places—pastures, fields, neglected areas, fencerows, and wastelands—but like poison ivy it is tough, vigorous, highly adaptable, and widely distributed, but with a preference for sandy soils. It grows as a bush, commonly about knee-high but sometimes almost waist-high to a man. Fortunately, it is easily recognized by those who pay attention to such things, as the stems and big, somewhat crinkled lobate leaves are visibly frosted with toxic prickles, and it does not closely resemble any other forbs with which it is usually associated. It is often partly concealed in the midst of other plants, however, including some very attractive wild flowers, and there it is more of a hazard.

In my growing-up days on the farm I helped hoe bull nettles out of gardens and fields and sometimes ate with relish their delicious, nutty-tasting seeds. Then and later I have had a few painful accidental encounters with them—one indelibly memorable. On a sweltering day in East Texas some years ago, I stumbled backwards onto a yard-high bull nettle—and launched myself aloft with several of its virulent leaves plastered like flypaper to the seat of my sweat-drenched pants. Since that time I tend to get carried away when talking about the torment bull nettle's fiery bristles can inflict. So it seems best that I quote the dispassionate comments on that subject by a couple of respected botanists: "Certainly one of the best-armed plants among Texas wildflowers," said Howard Irwin. "Probably the best naturally protected plants except the cacti," said Ellen Schulz.

Back in 1834, frontier Texas botanist Jean Louis Berlandier had an encounter with bull nettles somewhere between San Antonio and the Colorado River, and he entered a few words about them in his journal. He seemed

somewhat more impressed by their natural protection than either Irwin or Schulz: "Its large and palmate leaves are bristling with hairs whose stings produce an unbearable pain, following by a small inflammation which lessens only with time. It is said that on the places where animals have been stung their hair falls out, and I myself have seen a mule lose an eye because of an accident of that nature."

I would like to know the nature of the mule's "accident," for certainly animals learn to avoid bull nettle. My curiosity was recently aroused by hundreds of small clumps of ungrazed palatable grasses pockmarking the otherwise heavily grazed stubble in a large central Texas field where a bunch of grown steers had been pastured for several months. On closer examination of a number of the clumps, I found in each that the ungrazed grass was snuggling among the branches of one or more healthy bull nettles, and I noticed that no hoofprints, elsewhere abundant, were to be seen in any of the clumps. The steers had avoided touching the nettles with either mouthparts or feet. They knew about bull nettle virulence, probably having learned through painful experience, and they had learned to move freely about it without making actual contact—something which those who go afield in search of flowers or birds, or whatever, should also make sure to learn.

Back in the 1940's, in his delightful book *Adventures with a Texas Naturalist*, Roy Bedichek paid well-deserved tribute to the Texas Highway Department, and to highway commissions generally; they "are becoming more and more conscious of the arboretum value of the right of way and are taking pains to extend the range of natives [indigenous plants], especially of the ornamental ones," he said. And, after several pages of elaboration, he continued: "It is the most conscious work in con-servation of natural beauty on a grand scale that is being done at all, overshadowing in extent, as it certainly does in influence on the public mind, even park systems, state and national."

It would have pleased Mr. Bedichek if he had known then how much more our highways—and our state parks, too—would be expanded and improved in the years that have since come and gone. For the Parks and Wildlife Department keeps on acquiring and developing new state parks, and the Highway Department continues to improve in its efforts to preserve native flora, to make drab places gracious with wild flowers and shrubs, and to generally perform wonders for the traveling public.

Still, it seems that some of us are never satisfied. My concern is, and has been for years, for some things *outside* the right-of-way fences—specifically, for areas of extraordinary natural beauty, or natural historical significance, or both, that lie adjacent to and in easy viewing distance of the road, but which require leisurely, contemplative observation because they are much too diverse and intricate to be viewed to advantage from the window of a passing automobile. Here and there along the state's seventy thousand miles of highways are such floristically special places—it's anybody's guess how many—and some are associated with geological or other natural features which can add considerable interest. They are, in effect, full-scale outdoor natural history exhibits of much potential intellectual and esthetic value. Yet they are just sitting there, unknown, unused—going to waste. I would like to see them made known and available for viewing, through appropriate roadside markers and parking facilities, to travelers who care about such things and who derive nourishment of mind and spirit from looking on them with inquiring and receptive eyes.

In a speech to a Texas Museum Asso-

ciation group about twenty-five years ago I touched on essentially the idea I am discussing here. I talked about a few roadside areas of special interest I had observed in various parts of Texas and called those areas "potential travelers' exhibits"—and there was enough favorable response to encourage me to hang on to the idea for a time. One of the areas discussed was in the general vicinity of Sanderson. The foreground, adjacent to the highway, was a good example of native semiarid, shortgrass prairie, though at that time it was somewhat overgrazed and drouth-damaged. It had a considerable scattering of such characteristic flowering plants as yucca, sotol, prickly pear, and mesquite, all of which had been important subsistence plants for prehistoric Indians of that region. The principal feature of interest, however, was in the background, perhaps a long quarter-mile away. There, high up on a south-facing limestone bluff, but clearly visible from the highway, was the gaping, smoke-blackened entrance of a natural cave which had been used for centuries as a shelter by ancient southwestern Indians. What identified it as such was a long talus slope of burned rock, ashes, and other refuse trailing down the bluff from the shelter's entrance. It didn't take much imagination on the part of a viewer to visualize the countless fires that had burned there over the centuries—fires that had cooked the cave dwellers' food and dispelled the chill of their long winter nights.

I didn't then, and don't now, consider that site better than others that could be found. I mentioned it primarily as an example of one with year-round elements of interest—which I considered desirable in any possible travelers' exhibit. There are plenty of other semidesert plant communities along our western highways, but none that I had seen with this one's extra margin of interest. The Indians' rock shelter, and the native plants that helped sustain them—in plain view, and still

looking very much as they did when the Indians were there—provided a dramatic glimpse into the human prehistory of the region. And that, I thought, gave the site unusual distinction.

A comprehensive search for sites suitable for travelers' exhibits would amount to a state-wide natural history survey. And it would necessarily involve a considerable number of participants, though it seems likely that some experts would volunteer their services.

Where would they look? Obviously, many long stretches of highway have no such bordering attractions worthy of consideration. On many other stretches, construction of parking facilities would be impractical for any of a dozen legitimate reasons. But after eliminating those from consideration, many thousands of highway miles remain along which natural sites of exceptional interest could be found.

East Texas is extravagantly endowed with wild flowers, including many different kinds of flowering trees, shrubs, and forbs, and they often occur with other vegetation in well-defined plant communities—some on hilltops, some on well-drained slopes, and others on rich, moist soils of floodplains. Outstanding roadside examples of these communities, in my opinion, would make beautiful and meaningful exhibits. South Texas has great prickly pear flats, fine stands of "brush country" shrubs, such as the profusely flowering *huijillo*, and lovely colonies of water lilies and American lotus in the roadside playas southward from Kingsville.

Even the High Plains, where untilled land is scarce, has attractive areas of much natural historical significance. One that I never pass in daylight without stopping for a time to admire borders U.S. Highway 385 about six miles south of Spring Lake. There, a sizable and beautifully rolling dune field is naturally and effectively stabilized by a fine grove of

western soapberry and hackberry trees, with a dominant understory of silver-colored sagebrush (*Artemesia* sp.), which blankets the entire area. Wild plums, aromatic sumac, and perhaps other understory shrubs are also present. At times sunflowers, pink morning-glory, and other wild flowers appear at places among the sagebrush. It is a rare and meaningful site indeed—especially on the almost treeless plains.

If all such areas in the state could be identified, inventoried, and rated according to their potential value to the traveling public, perhaps in time the best of them could be converted into actual travelers' exhibits. We have called attention to notable human achievements with explanatory historical markers in adequate parking areas along our highways. Would it not be equally appropriate to call attention in a comparable way to examples of nature's special handiwork?

There can be no question that destruction of natural habitat is the greatest threat to the welfare of our native plants and animals. Nor can there be any question that such destruction continues from various abusive land use practices and from ongoing absorption of natural real estate through urban sprawl and the incredible expansion of industry of one kind or another around our cities. Still, there are reasons for optimism concerning the future welfare of most, if not quite all, the native plant and animal species now extant in Texas.

The significant forces now generally considered collectively as the environmental movement are directed toward conservation and restoration of the natural environment and tend to compensate for still active destructive forces. Of paramount importance in this undertaking, I think, is the steadily growing appreciation and concern on the part of the general public for flowers and birds and other things that make up our natural heritage. This support makes possible, or at least much easier, the laudable constructive enterprises of federal, state, and private agencies and even the work of such able and influential individuals as Lady Bird Johnson.

But apart from the environmental movement, as such, there are other causes for optimism. Substantial improvements in land-use practices by the livestock growing industry is an especially encouraging development, since that industry controls most of the state's remaining natural environment. Having seen the disastrous consequences to their ranges of sustained overgrazing by sheep and goats, Texas ranchers are more and more practicing pasture rotation. That is, they are resting their pastures from livestock from time to time to allow forage vegetation a chance to recover. And more importantly, they have drastically reduced the number of sheep from about 10.8 million in 1943 to 2.4 million in recent years, and the number of goats from 4.2 million in 1966 to about 1.4 million at present.

In certain heavily overstocked pastures, during the devastating seven-year drouth of the 1950's, sheep and goats skinned off every visible shred of herbaceous vegetation—grasses, flowering forbs, weeds, everything—leaving the thin, rocky soils as naked and sunbaked as a desert wasteland that must remain forever barren. But in at least some of these pastures that have since been "rested" at times and stocked only with cattle, native grasses and a rich variety of flowering forbs are making a remarkable recovery—a convincing and cheering testimony to nature's incredible recuperative power.

Paradoxical as it seems, another encouraging development is the burgeoning economic importance of wildlife hunting. Hunting—especially of big-game species—has become an immensely popular sport throughout the livestock growing regions, and many ranchers now derive an important supplemen-

tal income from sale of hunting leases on their land. It is said that in some years owners of prime game land have profited as much from the sale of hunting leases as from their normal livestock operations.

Along with native game animals, including deer, wild turkeys, and javelinas, several exotic species have been introduced on many large ranches and have become a major economic asset. And because it is absolutely necessary to maintain suitable wildlife habitat—meaning adequate wild forage plants and plenty of woody cover—to support such animals, the ranchers have a powerful incentive to improve the ecological conditions of their ranges. Wholesale eradication of prickly pear, lechuguilla, and other brush species, a practice formerly considered beneficial for livestock range, effectively destroys wildlife habitat. Consequently, intensive clearing, as well as heavy grazing by livestock, is now being curtailed.

I have contributed my part to the general lamentation about the good earth being buried beneath asphalt and concrete pavements and sediments of major impoundments. Those, of course, were futile protests. Our urbanized, mechanized, high-speed mode of existence makes a certain amount of such things essential. We cannot do without reservoirs or without paved highways, streets, and parking lots. And we are not about to do away with any of them, unless, perhaps, to replace them with bigger and better ones of the same kind. So it behooves us to accept inevitables with as much grace as we can muster and to console ourselves with thoughts of the benefits we de-

rive from highway pavements. Let us remind ourselves that they serve us far better in our comings and goings than would the good earth that lies beneath them, and that they shed rainfall into adjoining ditches, thereby irrigating wild flowers sown there for our enjoyment by nature and the Highway Department.

Perhaps it would help us further to recall a miracle that came to pass during World War II. After Hitler's bombers had blown sections of London's ancient pavements to smithereens, and the newly exposed earth had been revived by sun and rain, 126 species of wild flowers sprouted and grew from seeds that had lain dormant for centuries beneath the pavement slabs. So we have a basis for supposing that the good earth beneath our maze of highway pavements is preserving for posterity the seeds of the fine wild flowers that now grace our land.

And now, having soothed our worries about the good earth buried, let us direct our attention to the vastly larger areas that still remain unburied. There is a lot of unsullied nature to enjoy out there, and there is always a chance that we will be inspired to improve it a bit now and then and maybe find ways to help prevent its despoilation.

Legitimate causes for optimism concerning the natural environment and its native fauna and flora may already outweigh existing pessimistic issues. I believe that Texas will bloom for its future generations as it did for those of the past and as, even now, it blooms for us.

GLEN EVANS

PLATES

The leaves of the bird-foot violet (*Viola pedata*) are edible, and its flowers are used medicinally and as decorations, or made into wines or syrups. It is an East Texas flower, blooming from March through April. Sometimes it is two-toned, the upper petals purple and the lower ones a lighter lavender.

Globe mallow (*Sphaeralcea angustifolia*) is also known as sore-eye poppy or *mal de ojos*. Indians are said to have had various medicinal uses for it and to have chewed the stem as a kind of gum.

Another common name for the May-pop (*Passiflora incarnata*) is passion-flower, because some people have associated its appearance, near Easter, with the Christian Passion.

The flower of the blue larkspur (*Delphinium carolinianum*), a member of the crowfoot family, is easily recognized by the "spur" or hollow tube that extends from its base. A perennial of central and northeastern Texas, it does very well in wildflower plantings, but it also has toxic properties that can be fatal to cattle.

Opposite: Water hyacinth (*Eichhornia crassipes*), though beautiful, is a noxious weed that clogs waterways and chokes out other wildlife and vegetation.

Red buckeye (*Aesculus pavia* var. *pavia*), an excellent yard tree for its showy red flowers and foliage, is also known as the horse chestnut because of its large, smooth, dark brown seeds. The flowers, which appear from March through May on hillsides of eastern Texas, have an irresistible appeal to hummingbirds.

The yellow flowers of the javelina bush (*Condalia ericoides*) are abundant in the Trans-Pecos area and are also found from the Brazos to the Red River. The Latin word in this species name, *ericoides*, refers to the shrub's tiny leaves, which make it easily identifiable.

The pitcher-plant (*Sarracenia alata*) was originally described in 1700, and its name was accepted by Linnaeus in 1737. Several different insects live in the leaf tubes, feeding their larvae upon the leaf tissue or the dead insects captured in the plant's tubes.

Opposite: Chisos bluebonnet (*Lupinus havardii*), the West Texas lupine, is included with its two eastern relatives as the Texas state flower. It is one of the earliest flowers to appear in the Big Bend region.

Albinos are rare among bluebonnets (*Lupinus* sp.), but
they do occur, and a few such
white individuals may be
found scattered in the fields
of blue that blanket Texas
roadsides in the spring.

Marsh rose-gentian (*Sabatia dodecandra* var. *foli-
osa*), also known as a marsh-pink, is found in open
wet woodlands, around ponds, and along the edges
of streams or ditches.

Contrary to what many think, the wild
azalea shrub (*Rhododendron canes-
cens*) is no relation to the honeysuckle
vine, despite a similar appearance and
fragrance.

Opposite: Purple iris (*Iris virginica*), also known
by the common name southern blue flag, is found
along watercourses and in wetland environments
in eastern and southeastern Texas.

Overleaf: Bluebonnets and Indian paintbrush.

37

Widow's tears (*Commelina* sp.) is a dayflower usually found in damp, shady places. Each blossom remains open for only one morning. On one plant near Austin, new blossoms have been seen to appear each morning for more than ten weeks, with as many as fourteen a day.

Flowers of many colors brighten Texas roadsides in the spring and summer.

Opposite: Also known as mescal bean because of its hard, thick-walled seed pods, Texas mountain laurel (*Sophora secundiflora*) occurs from the Edwards Plateau south and west to the Trans-Pecos.

Dalea (*Dalea frutescens*), a shrub, is named for
an eighteenth-century English botanist, Samuel
Dale. It can be found in central and southern
Texas, where it flowers in late summer.

The leaves of the legume sensitive brier (*Schrankia* sp.) close during cloudy weather or when it is touched. Another common name for it is shame boy.

Lion-heart (*Physostegia digitalis*), a member of the mint family, is found in eastern Texas. It is also called obedient plant, because the flowers, when moved about, remain in the position in which they are placed. Another common name is dragon-head.

Flowers of the butterfly pea vine (*Centrosema virginianum*) may be seen in the eastern half of the state. Wild fowl, especially doves and quail, are fond of the seeds. The flowers appear in the summer.

In some areas in southern Texas entire fields are covered with herbertia (*Alophia drummondii*), creating the illusion of blue water in a lake.

There are a number of species of blue-eyed grass
(*Sisyrinchium* sp.), which is not a grass but an iris
that appears from the Gulf to the High Plains. The
species are sometimes difficult to distinguish.

Evening primrose (*Oenothera speciosa*) is one of our most common wild flowers, blooming along many miles of Texas highways in mid- to late spring.

Bluebell gentian (*Eustoma exaltatum*), a native of southern Texas, remains fresh for long periods after cutting, and it is gathered by florists and sold with cut flowers. Unfortunately it is disappearing in many areas.

Opposite: One of the most common Texas wild flowers, evening primrose (*Oenothera speciosa*) occurs throughout the state. It is our only pink evening primrose. Others are white or yellow (the latter are called buttercups). In the northern parts of the state the flowers tend to be white and are evening-opening, whereas further south the blossoms are more likely to be colored and open in the morning.

The fruit of the prairie rose (*Rosa* sp.), called a "hip," is an excellent source of Vitamin C, and rose hips are often used in teas and jellies. The rose petals are dried and used for their fragrance. More than a dozen species of wild roses bloom in Texas, and they are particularly abundant in the northeastern part of the state.

Gay feather (*Liatris* sp.), one of our showiest natives, usually occurs in large colonies of plants. It can be domesticated easily and is often known as blazing stars. Many species of this genus have medicinal uses.

Flowers of the grass-pink (*Calopogon pulchellus*) and other members of the orchid family are marvelously adapted to pollination by insects. Their seeds are the smallest known, being microscopic in size, and they will not germinate unless fungi are present in the humus where the minute seeds come to rest. From the hundreds of thousands of seeds that an orchid flower produces, only a very few ever grow into new plants.

The tiny, soft, gray leaves of the cenizo (*Leuco-phyllum* sp.), also spelled ceniza or senizo, blend well with its dry, rocky surroundings in South and West Texas, but in late summer, usually after a rain or when the humidity is high, the plants burst into color with bright pink, purple, or blue flowers.

Rose pogonia (*Pogonia ophi-oglossoides*), an inch-long or-chid also called snake-mouth, raises solitary flowers among the savanna grasses of eastern and southeastern Texas in April, May, and June.

Opposite: A rare jewel of the Big Thicket, the grass-pink (*Calopogon pulchellus*), or calopogon orchid, is losing ground fast to destruction of its habitat and to wild-flower pickers.

Two species of the umbrellawort (*Allionia* sp.) may be found in Texas. They are members of the four-o'clock family, which includes the tropical bougainvilleas.

Opposite: The spine-armed leaves of this beautiful flower clearly indicate why it is called prickly poppy (*Argemone* sp.).

In addition to beautiful flowers, the pitaya cactus (*Echinocereus enneacanthus*) produces fruit with a fragrance and flavor resembling strawberries and which may be eaten fresh or made into preserves.

Herbertia (*Alophia drummondii*), also called prairie iris, is the only species of this flower in Texas. It is limited in range to the prairies and grasslands of southern Texas, where it is commonly found in large colonies.

Many kinds of phlox (*Phlox* sp.) contribute their colors to Texas fields and roadsides in the spring. Shades range from red through purple to blue.

Several different species of Spiderworts (*Trade-scantia* sp.) grow in the state, and they often hybridize, making identification difficult. Their light blue to purple flowers bloom throughout the spring in open, sunny areas.

Of the thirty or so species of skeleton weed (*Lygo-desmia* sp.) in North America, four are Texas natives. They may be found mainly on the higher plains and prairies and in the Trans-Pecos, and they are summer bloomers.

Actually a member of the iris family, the purple pleat-leaf (*Eustylis purpurea*) is also called the pinewoods lily and may be found in grassy areas in eastern and southern Texas.

The tiny flowers of blue-curls (*Phacelia congesta*) may be found, often in large patches, along road-sides and in sandy or rocky fields throughout the state except the eastern counties.

Opposite: Thick stands of phlox (foreground) and red prickly poppies illuminate a roadside near Floresville.

The hedgehog or pitaya cactus (*Echinocereus enneacanthus*) grows throughout the counties from the Edwards Plateau to the Trans-Pecos. Its strawberry-flavored fruit may be eaten fresh or as preserves.

Texas mountain laurel (*Sophora secundiflora*), a beautiful evergreen shrub with showy purple flowers, is a star of the springtime display in the West Texas plateaus and Trans-Pecos mountains.

Known both as the Mexican buckeye (*Ungnadia speciosa*) and Texas buckeye, this shrub or small tree appears most frequently west of the Brazos River. Its showy flowers and leaves make it an exceptionally beautiful ornamental. Its seeds were used by the Indians in their ceremonial rattles or as beads and other decorations.

Violet wood-sorrel (*Oxalis violacea*) blooms in early spring when its leaves appear and then again in the fall after its leaves are gone.

The showy, easily cultivated gay feather (*Liatris* sp.) produces flowers along a slender spike which begins opening at the tip. The plant makes spectacular displays, for it almost always forms large colonies, blooming in the summer and fall.

Cholla (*Opuntia imbricata* var. *imbricata*), also called cane cholla, is closely related to the prickly pears, though it looks quite different. The cholla, which may grow eight or nine feet tall, has cylindrical, dull green branches, whereas the prickly pear has flattened pads.

Three species of cenizo (*Leucophyllum* sp.), also called Texas silverleaf, whiteleaf, purple sage, or Texas sage, grow in Texas. Cenizo normally blooms in the fall, but its blossoms can also appear almost any month of the year after a good rain. Its range is west and south of San Antonio to the Trans-Pecos and Big Bend country. Because of its attractive blossoms and foliage, cenizo is becoming increasingly popular as a cultivated ornamental shrub.

Rock lettuce (*Pinaropappus roseus*), a spring flower, is common to central Texas and varies in color from white to pale pink. Another common name is white dandelion.

Dandelion (*Taraxacum erythrospermum*), probably one of the most common flowers in the world, is an humble European native that does well in much of Texas, producing showy puffs of color from early spring into June. Its leaves make salad and wine. In this photograph the flower has faded away, and the white seeds are ready to fly away at the slightest breeze or a child's breath.

The fruit of the elderberry (*Sambucus canadensis*) can be used in jams or made into wine. The flowers sometimes blossom in late spring and then again in late summer. A moisture-loving plant, elderberry is commonly found growing at the edge of ponds and streams.

Different specimens of prickly poppy (*Argemone* sp.) have flowers of various colors from white to deep red and lavender. Because of their fragile petals and spiny leaves and stems, they are best observed rather than gathered for bouquets.

Torrey yucca (*Yucca torreyi*), named for John Torrey, a prominent nineteenth-century botanist, is found on mesas and hillsides of the upper Rio Grande Plains, Edwards Plateau, and Trans-Pecos regions. Here, lavender verbena grows in the foreground.

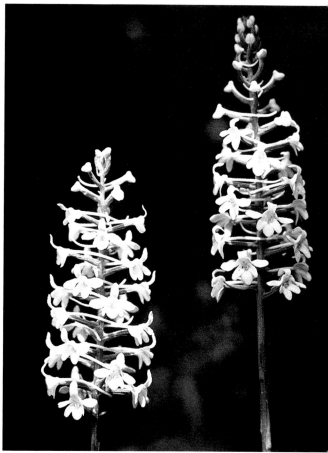

Snowy orchids (*Habenaria nivea*) light up bogs, wet prairies, and soggy savannas in the Big Thicket from May through August. The flowers are tiny—to three-eighths of an inch long—and may be distinguished from their close relatives by their lip, which is in the uppermost position.

Charles Darwin was the first to prove that the small butterwort (*Pinguicula pumila*) is carnivorous. Its leaves first trap insects on their sticky upper surface, then roll their edges over to enclose and digest their prey.

An inhabitant of the Guadalupe Moutains, rock
mat (*Petrophytum caespitosum*), also called rock
spiraea, is a member of the rose family and thrives
in barren limestone crevices at altitudes above
three thousand feet.

Rain lilies (*Cooperia drummondii*) blossom during the summer, most often after a heavy rain. They bloom overnight and usually last only one day.

Three species of white-topped umbrella grass (*Dichromena* sp.), a tufted perennial which actually is not a grass but a sedge, occur in Texas; two grow in the west, and one is found in the southeast.

Found only in the Big Thicket, silky camellia (*Stewartia malacodendron*) grows along streams and on wooded hillsides.

Wild morning glory (*Ipomoea trichocarpa*), though a lovely flower, can be a problem for farmers. Once it gets established, it is difficult to get rid of.

Spider-lily (*Hymenocallis liriosme*) flowers are very fragrant. An inhabitant of low, moist, semishaded areas, the spider-lily can be successfully domesticated if given enough water.

Beach morning-glory (*Ipomoea purpurea*) can be seen in the dunes along the Gulf shoreline from spring through fall. Sensitive to sunlight, its flowers open each morning and close in the afternoon. Specially adapted to life on the sand, it spreads by a net of running vines that anchors the dunes in place.

Several species and varieties of the lazy daisy (*Aphanostephus* sp.), little relatives of the sunflower, grow in Texas. They range in color from white to reddish purple, but they are never yellow. Their name perhaps derives from their habit of "sleeping in"; their flowers do not open until late morning.

The beautiful, fragrant flowers of the bull nettle (*Cnidoscolus texanus*) belie its true nature, for its leaves and stems are densely covered with thousands of fine toxic prickles, which are intensely painful to touch. Driven by hunger, cattle, goats, and deer will eat prickly pear despite its cruel spines and glochids, but they will leave bull nettle quite untouched.

The water-lily (*Nymphaea odorata*) is a familiar flower of spring and summer ponds and still streams in eastern and coastal Texas. Each flower lasts only one day.

The small rain lilies (*Cooperia* sp.), of six or seven species, have the habit of shooting up their blooms a day or two after heavy fall or sometimes spring rains. The flowers last for only a few days before withering.

In a scene typical of eastern Texas, weathered fenceposts and stately eastern red cedars frame a field sparking with tiny white wild flowers.

Eight different species of prickly poppies (*Argemone* sp.) are native to Texas. The most common are found in old fields and the disturbed grounds of abandoned farmsteads and barnyards.

Opposite: One of the .earliest heralds of spring in eastern Texas, the fine tracery of dogwood (*Cornus florida*) blossoms brightens the dark woods. The thickly spaced blossoms are especially conspicuous because of their large size and because they normally appear before the leaves.

Bluebonnets (*Lupinus* sp.) and pink evening primroses (*Oenothera* sp.) cover the ground in front of
live oaks near LaGrange.

Bluebonnets (*Lupinus* sp.) and white prickly poppies (*Argemone* sp.) decorate an old well near La Vernia.

The common name for the longspur columbine (*Aquilegia longissima*) comes from the Latin word *columba*, meaning "dove," while its scientific genus name, *Aquilegia*, is derived from another Latin word, *aquila*, meaning "eagle." In Texas it is found only near springs in the canyons of the Chisos Mountains in Big Bend National Park.

Opposite: It is unusual to find a flower of a stick-leaf (*Mentzelia* sp.), since the blooms of many species open either late in the day or at night. This flower was photographed in an area of restored native prairie re-created by the Texas Parks and Wildlife Department at Caprock Canyons State Park.

The yellow-flowered Jimmy-weed (*Isocoma wrightii*) is common on some alkali plains of far West Texas and the Trans-Pecos.

A patch of yellow coreopsis (*Coreopsis* sp.) blooms among other wild flowers, including Indian paint-brush and pink evening primrose, along a fence in central Texas.

The vivid yellow blossoms of this evening primrose (*Oenothera* sp.) give it the common name "buttercup." These flowers were photographed near Floresville.

Overleaf: Yellow coreopsis, or golden wave, and scattered white daisies decorate a shoreline of Falcon Reservoir in far South Texas.

The cut-leaved daisy (*Engelmannia pinnatifida*) is a common wild flower throughout all but eastern Texas. It blooms in open country from spring to early summer.

Sunflowers (*Helianthus* sp.) of many species grow
throughout Texas and are among the best known
and most popular of wild flowers.

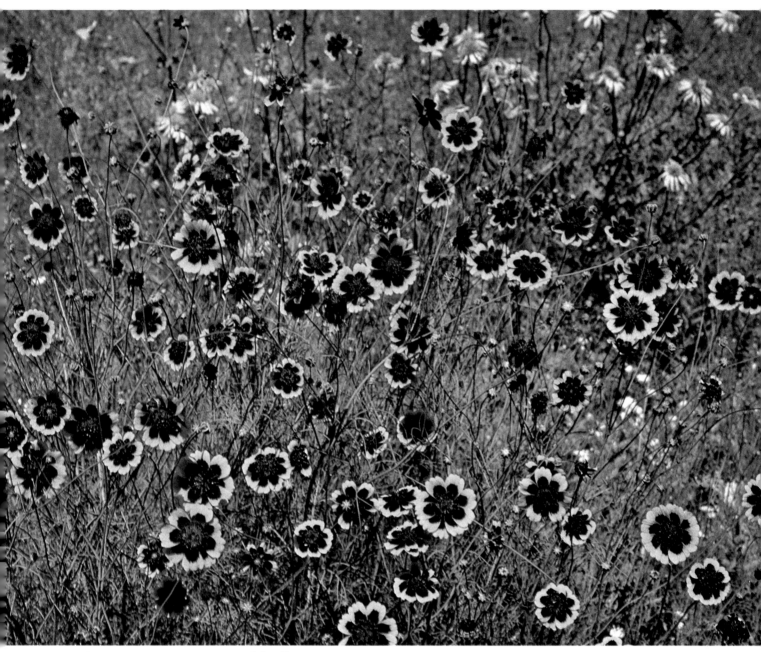

Coreopsis (*Coreopsis* sp.), sometimes solid yellow and sometimes, like these flowers, with reddish brown centers, is also called tick-seed because its seeds cling to clothing and the hair of animals.

Overleaf: A fine scattering of wild flowers decorates the canyon rim at Caprock Canyons State Park in Briscoe County.

Huisache (*Acacia farnesiana*), also called sweet
acacia because of the fragrance of its small, ball-
shaped flowers, grows up to thirty feet tall, sometimes in dense thickets, in some parts of South
Texas.

Black brush (*Acacia rigidula*) is similar to its close relative huisache, but black brush flowers are whiter, grow in elongated spikes, and bloom earlier in the spring.

The fragrant, bright yellow huisache (pronounced "we-satch") was once cultivated to provide oils for French perfumes.

Opposite: Golden wave (*Coreopsis* sp.) decorates an old farmhouse near Union Hill in western Washington County.

The flower of the partridge-pea (*Cassia fasciculata*) closes or withers about midday, and the plant's leaves partially close when touched. Partridge-pea is a member of the legume family. The seeds are important food for game birds, and the plant is sometimes included in soil improvement cover crops, but it is said to be toxic to livestock when it is eaten green.

Opposite: During World War II, floss from butterfly-weed (*Asclepias tuberosa*), with the red flowers, was used as filler for life preservers and flying suits. It is five or six times as bouyant as cork, warmer than wool, and much lighter than either of those substances. Cordage can be made from the plant's stems, and oil can be extracted from its seeds. Young pods can be boiled and eaten. The plant's roots give it another common name: pleurisy root.

Cowpen daisy (*Verbesina encelioides*), also called butter daisy, is a beautiful annual that often occurs in large numbers. When disturbed, it gives off an unpleasant odor. It can be domesticated easily and is a favorite nectar and pollen source for butterflies and other insects.

A most beautiful native vine, cross-vine (*Bignonia capreolata*) gets its name from the fact that the multicolored cells in its stem are arranged in the shape of a cross. Its flowers have the fragrance of fresh coffee.

Bladderworts (*Utricularia* sp.) can be found only in the eastern part of the state, and they comprise one of the four carnivorous genera that are native Texans. The plants may be either rooted on the ground or more commonly floating in water, and their underground or submerged stems have small, buoyant, bladderlike organs that catch and digest tiny insects and water plants.

Water-spider orchid (*Habenaria repens*) grows on floating mats of vegetation along the edges of lakes and ponds, blooming from May until December.

Carolina jessamine (*Gelsemium sempervirens*) is one of our most beautiful native vines. However, all parts of this plant have toxic properties that can be fatal. Pleasantly fragrant and easily cultivated, it makes a most attractive addition to a wild-flower garden.

The lovely yellow flowers of velvet-leaf mallow (*Wissadula holosericea*) appear in the fall.

Opposite: Sneezeweed (*Helenium autumnale*), a member of the sunflower family, is usually found in north central and eastern Texas. It may be distinguished from the brown-eyed susan by its smaller, fringed flowers and narrower leaves.

Rock-nettle (*Eucnide bartonioides*) flowers are found in the lower canyons of the Rio Grande downriver from the Big Bend. They are also native to limestone cliffs of the western Edwards Plateau.

A member of the orchid family, the small, inconspicuous green adder's mouth (*Malaxis unifolia*) is sometimes found in eastern Texas, growing along moist wooded slopes and the edges of streams in forests of pines mixed with hardwoods. Its tiny flowers open from March through July.

Carolina-lily (*Lilium michauxii*), also called the wood lily, is one of only two true lilies that occur in Texas. Its natural range includes the pine-oak woodlands of southeastern Texas, but it is hard to find.

Japanese honeysuckle (*Lonicera japonica*), a native of Asia, has escaped from cultivation to become an obnoxious weed threatening native vegetation. It covers the ground in thick, tangled mats or climbs into shrubs and trees, eventually killing its support. It makes good browse for deer.

From midsummer until Halloween the yellow-fringed orchid (*Habenaria ciliaris*) blooms in the grassy flatlands and savannas of the Big Thicket.

The large inflated lip of the lady's slipper orchid (*Cypripedium calceolus*) gives it its common name. It has the largest flowers of any native orchid in Texas. It is what botanists call a circumferal species, as its range extends around the world in the Northern Hemisphere.

Opposite: Many will recognize golden wave (*Coreopsis* sp.) by another common name, tick-seed, or its scientific name, coreopsis. It flourishes in domestic gardens in America and Europe as well as in the wild.

Despite its lovely yellow flower, poison bitterweed (*Hymenoxys scaposa*) is toxic to sheep that are tempted by it during times of scant rainfall.

Brown-eyed Susan (*Rudbeckia hirta*) is a member of the aster family. The word *hirta* in its scientific name means "rough" or "shaggy" and refers to the bristly hairs on the plant. It is one of the most common summer wild flowers in the eastern two-thirds of Texas.

Bur marigold (*Bidens laevis*), another common name for which is sugar ticks, is an annual or perennial herb that grows best near water. The barbs on the fruit of the plant can become attached to clothing or the fur of animals.

Bright yellow flowers of the sunflower family add a touch of vivid color to a dry West Texas canyon.

The flowers of the coneflower (*Rudbeckia* sp.) are found in many American and European domestic gardens. Many insects are attracted to them. Where there is enough moisture, the flowers will bloom throughout the summer months. They are widely distributed in Texas.

The heads of sunflowers (*Helianthus* sp.) are rich in pollen and nectar that attract a variety of insects. Some sunflowers also provide oil, food, cordage, and dye for commercial use. The common sunflower is among the most widespread of native American flowers—so much so that it has been suggested as the national flower. An amazingly adaptable plant, it grows throughout Texas and blossoms from spring to fall.

Opposite: Five species of silphium (*Silphium* sp.) are found in north central, central, and eastern Texas. All of them hybridize and intergrade with each other. Another common name for them is rosin-weed.

More than a dozen species and varieties of prickly pear cactus (*Opuntia* sp.) grow in Texas. Most have yellow flowers, though the flowers of some are red or partly red. The flattened pads of prickly pears are actually the plants' stems adapted to their dry environment; they have no leaves.

Mesa greggii (*Nerisyrenia camporum*), a tiny member of the mustard family, grows in western Texas and is seen here growing within the foliage of a lechuguilla.

Antelope-horn (*Asclepias viridis*), also called green milkweed, occurs over much of the state but is most commonly seen in eastern Texas. In common with many other members of the milkweed family, it contains a milky juice. It blooms throughout the summer.

Odorless onion (*Nothoscordium bivalve*), a member of the lily family, is similar to the wild onion but without the onion odor or taste. Other common names are crow poison and false garlic.

Overleaf: Torrey yucca (*Yucca torreyi*) is named in honor of the American botanist John Torrey, and it has many uses. A water source during droughts, it also provides food for humans, animals, and insects. This yucca is abundant and widespread, especially in the Trans-Pecos region, where it can be seen blooming at one place or another every month of the year. Another common name for it is old shag.

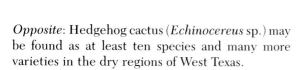

Opposite: Hedgehog cactus (*Echinocereus* sp.) may be found as at least ten species and many more varieties in the dry regions of West Texas.

113

About twenty species of yucca (*Yucca* sp.) grow in Texas. These dry-country members of the lily family were widely used for food and fiber by the Indians of the Southwest.

The Texas madrone (*Arbutus xalapensis*) is also called lady's leg or naked Indian because its thin outer bark peels off in papery sheets, leaving the trunk and limbs exposed. In central Texas this beautiful tree is becoming rare—if not, indeed, endangered—because of browsing by deer and rabbits, which seem to savor its inner bark.

Overleaf: Often called by its scientific name, acacia, huisache (*Acacia farnesiana*) has an erratic blooming pattern, sometimes beginning as early as late December. The yellow flowers have a great attraction for honeybees. Here, a golden bush blazes behind a stand of winecups, evening primroses, paintbrushes, and other wild flowers.

Yellow wild flowers decorate a roadside near an old farm between Winedale and Round Top in Fayette County.

The lovely blossoms of a claret-cup cactus (*Echinocereus triglochidiatus*) soften the harshness of this Trans-Pecos landscape.

Red prickly poppies (*Argemone sanguinea*) thrive on old plowed ground on a farm near Floresville.

Indian paintbrushes (*Castilleja indivisa*), sown by the Texas Highway Department, enliven a roadside near Caldwell.

The very small greenish yellow flowers of Indian paintbrush (*Castilleja indivisa*) are nearly obscured by large spatula-shaped bracts that vary in color from white to pale pink to orange or scarlet. The plant cannot be easily transplanted, but it does grow readily from seed.

Overleaf: Pink evening primrose (*Oenothera* sp.), one of our most common wild flowers, lends its delicate beauty to a Texas landscape.

The lush-flowered claret-cup cactus (*Echinocereus triglochidiatus*) may be seen blooming in hilly and mountainous country throughout southwestern Texas.

Opposite: Red prickly poppies (*Argemone sanguinea*) spread their deep red blossoms over an old field near Floresville.

Claret-cups (*Echinocereus triglochidiatus*) glow in
the sunlight along the rim of a ravine near Langtry.

Red prickly poppies (*Argemone sanguinea*) brighten the farmlands of central and southwestern Texas in early spring.

Overleaf: Crimson clover (*Trifolium incarnatum*), a native of southern Europe escaped from cultivation in this country, is now widespread along roadsides and in fields throughout the eastern half of the state.

More often the flowers of the yellow lotus (*Nelumbo lutea*) are pale yellow. After the flower has bloomed, its seed pods are often used in dried flower arrangements. The Indians made flour from the dried plant and roasted and ate its seeds. The flowers may be found raised slightly above the surface of quiet waters in eastern and southern Texas.

Turk's cap (*Malvaviscus arboreus* var. *drummon-dii*), a semishrub also called Texas mallow, flowers throughout the year in its southern range. Its fruit resembles tiny apples. It is a member of the mallow family, which also includes cotton, okra, and the hibiscuses.

Carolina snailseed (*Cocculus carolinus*), a vine, is found throughout the state. It is also called moonseed vine, red-berried moonseed, and coral berry. It is not poisonous as is popularly supposed, and because it is easily grown, it is ideal for yards and gardens. Male and female flowers appear on separate plants, and only the female flowers will bear fruit. The common name moonseed vine derives from its crescent- or "moon"-shaped seeds.

Phlox (*Phlox* sp.) flowers are common to most Texas roadsides. There are more than fifty species of phlox in North America, with twelve species and several subspecies in this state, and various species form hybrids.

The redbud (*Cercis canadensis*) is known to have been cultivated since 1641. Fluid extracted from the bark is purported to have medicinal value as a treatment for dysentery. Its seeds and foliage provide browse and nourishment for deer and various birds. The flowers appear usually in February or early March before the leaves set on.

While most flowers in the legume family are designed for pollination by bees, those of the coral bean (*Erythrina herbacea*) are colored various shades of bright red and are more attractive to hummingbirds. Occurring naturally in Texas only in the coastal and extreme eastern regions, this attractive flower flourishes in gardens in other parts of the state.

Annual sundew (*Drosera annua*) is one of the few insect-eating plants to be found in Texas. Growing in soils that are poor in nutrient substances, it subsists on small insects that become entangled in sticky tentacles on the leaves at the base of the plant. The sundew's botanical name is derived from the Greek word for dew and refers to the glistening drops of moisture that trap the insects.

Indian blanket (*Gaillardia pulchella*), a bright, multi-colored beauty, is one of our most admired common wild flowers, often found in extensive colonies along highways and in fields throughout Texas in spring and early summer. It is also called gaillardia and fire-wheel, and it is often cultivated in this country and in Europe.

Opposite: Coral honeysuckle (*Lonicera sempervirens*), an attractive Texas native, climbs on nearby vegetation but never becomes thick and unmanageable like its Asian counterpart, Japanese honeysuckle. It is an excellent source of nectar for hummingbirds, butterflies, and other insects.

The common name of the Mexican hat (*Ratibida columnaris*) comes from its appearance, which reminds one of a sombrero. It and its close relatives are found throughout Texas.

A native species that is often cultivated, lantana (*Lantana* sp.) is very resistant to hot, dry weather. Its only fault is an unpleasant odor that it emits when its foliage is crushed.

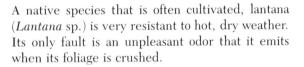

An old hay rake stands surrounded by bluebonnets and Indian paintbrush in a farmyard near Stockdale.

Opposite: Coreopsis (*Coreopsis* sp.), also called tick-seed, is a common Texas wild flower, growing throughout most of the state. About nine species may be found here.

Overleaf: The century plant (*Agave americana*) belies its name, for it does not live for a hundred years but normally for less than twenty. It invariably dies after flowering and fruiting. Various species and forms of this plant grow throughout southern and Trans-Pecos Texas.

141

PHOTOGRAPHIC CREDITS

Frontispiece: *Jack Lewis*

Page(s):

32:	top left, *Bob Parvin*; top right, *John Suhrstedt*; bottom left, *Jim Harris*; bottom right, *Jack Lewis*
33:	*Greg White*
34:	top left, *Jack Lewis*; top right, bottom, *Bob Parvin*
35:	*Robert Carr*
36:	*Bob Parvin*
37:	top left, *Stephan Myers*; top right, *Jack Lewis*; bottom, *John Suhrstedt*
38–39:	*Jack Lewis*
40:	*Jack Lewis*
41:	top, *Glen Evans*; bottom, *Jack Lewis*
42:	*Robert Carr*
43:	top left, *George Oxford Miller*; top right, bottom left, *Jack Lewis*; bottom right, *Bob Parvin*
44:	*Bob Parvin*
45:	*Jack Lewis*
46:	*John Suhrstedt*
47:	*Phillip Malnassy*
48:	left, *Greg White*; right, *George Oxford Miller*
49:	*Geyata Ajilvsgi*
50:	*Jim Bones*
51:	top, *Charles Carlson*; bottom, *Geyata Ajilvsgi*
52:	*Randy Green*
53:	*Randy Green*
54:	*Jack Lewis*
55:	top, bottom, *Jack Lewis*
56:	*Jack Lewis*
57:	all, *Jack Lewis*
58:	top, *Jack Lewis*; bottom, *Glen Evans*
59:	*Jack Lewis*
60:	top, *Bob Parvin*; bottom, *John Suhrstedt*
61:	*Greg White*
62:	top, bottom, *Jack Lewis*
63:	top, bottom, *Charles Carlson*
64:	*Jack Lewis*
65:	top, *Jack Lewis*; bottom, *Glen Evans*
66:	*Stephan Myers*
67:	top left, *Randy Green*; top right, *Geyata Ajilvsgi*; bottom, *John Suhrstedt*
68:	*George Oxford Miller*
69:	top, *John Suhrstedt*; bottom, *Jack Lewis*
70:	*Phillip Malnassy*
71:	all, *Jack Lewis*
72:	top left, top right, bottom right, *Jack Lewis*; bottom left, *Randy Green*
73:	*Jack Lewis*
74:	*Jack Lewis*
75:	*Jack Lewis*
76:	*Jack Lewis*
77:	*Jack Lewis*
78:	*Jack Lewis*
79:	*Randy Green*
80:	*Randy Green*
81:	*Randy Green*
82–83:	*Jack Lewis*
84–85:	*Randy Green*
86:	*Glen Evans*
87:	*Jack Lewis*
88–89:	*Jack Lewis*
90–91:	*Randy Green*
92:	*Jack Lewis*
93:	*Jack Lewis*
94:	*Jack Lewis*
95:	*Randy Green*
96:	*Jack Lewis*
97:	*Jack Lewis*
98:	*George Oxford Miller*
99:	top left, bottom right, *Betty Allison Cawlfield*; top right, *Bob Parvin*; bottom left, *Geyata Ajilvsgi*
100:	*Greg White*
101:	*George Oxford Miller*
102:	top left, *Geyata Ajilvsgi*; top right, *Jim Bones*; bottom, *Phillip Malnassy*
103:	*Jack Lewis*
104:	left, *Phillip Malnassy*; right, *Geyata Ajilvsgi*
105:	*Jack Lewis*